TAO TE CHING

Tao Te Ching

A New English Version,
with Foreword and Notes,
by Stephen Mitchell

HarperPerennial
A Division of HarperCollins*Publishers*

A hardcover edition of this book was published by
Harper & Row in 1988.

First HarperPerennial edition published 1991.

Designer: David Bullen

*The Library of Congress has catalogued the hardcover
edition as follows:*

Lao-tzu.
    Tao te ching.

    Translation of: Tao te ching.
    I. Mitchell, Stephen, 1943–
II. Title.
BL1900.L26E5   1988   299'.51482   88-45123
ISBN 0-06-016001-2
ISBN 0-06-091608-7 (pbk.)

91 92 93 94 95 RRD 10 9 8 7 6 5 4 3 2

TO VICKI

Who can find a good woman?
She is precious beyond all things.
Her husband's heart trusts her completely.
She is his best reward.

PROV. 31:10–11

Foreword

Tao Te Ching (pronounced, more or less, *Dow Deh Jing*) can be translated as *The Book of the Immanence of the Way* or *The Book of the Way and of How It Manifests Itself in the World* or, simply, *The Book of the Way*. Since it is already well known by its Chinese title, I have let that stand.

About Lao-tzu, its author, there is practically nothing to be said. He may have been an older contemporary of Confucius (551–479 B.C.E.) and may have held the position of archive-keeper in one of the petty kingdoms of the time. But all the information that has come down to us is highly suspect. Even the meaning of his name is uncertain (the most likely interpretations: "the Old Master" or, more picturesquely, "the Old Boy"). Like an Iroquois woodsman, he left no traces. All he left us is his book: the classic manual on the art of living, written in a style of gemlike lucidity, radiant with humor and grace and largeheartedness and deep wisdom: one of the wonders of the world.

People usually think of Lao-tzu as a hermit, a dropout from society, dwelling serenely in some mountain hut, unvisited except perhaps by the occasional traveler arriving from a '60s joke to ask, "What is the meaning of life?" But it's clear from his teachings that he deeply cared about society, if society means the welfare of one's fellow human beings; his book is, among other things, a treatise on the art of government, whether of a country or of a child. The misperception may arise from his insistence on *wei wu wei*, literally "doing not-doing," which has been seen as passivity. Nothing could be further from the truth.

A good athlete can enter a state of body-awareness in which the right stroke or the right movement happens by itself, effortlessly, without any interference of the conscious will. This is a paradigm for non-action: the purest and most effective form of action. The game plays the game; the poem writes the poem; we can't tell the dancer from the dance.

> Less and less do you need to force things,
> until finally you arrive at non-action.
> When nothing is done,
> nothing is left undone.

Nothing is done because the doer has wholeheartedly vanished into the deed; the fuel has been completely transformed into flame. This "nothing" is, in fact, everything. It happens when we trust the intelligence of the universe in the same way that an athlete or a dancer trusts the superior intelligence of the body. Hence Lao-tzu's emphasis on softness. Softness means the opposite of rigidity, and is synonymous with suppleness, adaptability, endurance. Anyone who has seen a tai ch'i or aikido master doing not-doing will know how powerful this softness is.

Lao-tzu's central figure is a man or woman whose life is in perfect harmony with the way things are. This is not an idea; it is a reality; I have seen it. The Master has mastered Nature; not in the sense of conquering it, but of becoming it. In surrendering to the Tao, in giving up all concepts, judgments, and desires, her mind has grown naturally compassionate. She finds deep in her own experience the central truths of the art of living, which are paradoxical only on the surface: that the more truly solitary we are, the more compassionate we can be; the more we let go of what we love, the more present our love becomes; the clearer our insight into what is beyond good and evil, the more we can embody the good. Until finally she is able to say, in all humility, "I am the Tao, the Truth, the Life."

The teaching of the Tao Te Ching is moral in the deepest sense. Unencumbered by any concept of sin, the Master doesn't see evil as a force to resist, but simply as an opaqueness, a state of self-absorption which is in disharmony with the universal process, so that, as with a dirty window, the light can't shine through. This freedom from moral categories allows him his great compassion for the wicked and the selfish.

> Thus the Master is available to all people
> and doesn't reject anyone.
> He is ready to use all situations
> and doesn't waste anything.
> This is called embodying the light.
>
> What is a good man but a bad man's teacher?
> What is a bad man but a good man's job?
> If you don't understand this, you will get lost,
> however intelligent you are.
> It is the great secret.

The reader will notice that in the many passages where Lao-tzu describes the Master, I have used the pronoun "she" at least as often as "he." The Chinese language doesn't make this kind of distinction; in English we have to choose. But since we are all, potentially, the Master (since the Master is, essentially, us), I felt it would be untrue to present a male archetype, as other versions have, ironically, done. Ironically, because of all the great world religions the teaching of Lao-tzu is by far the most female. Of course, you should feel free, throughout the book, to substitute "he" for "she" or vice versa.

As to method: I worked from Paul Carus's literal version, which provides English equivalents (often very quaint ones) alongside each of the Chinese ideograms. I also consulted dozens of translations into English, German, and French. But the most essential preparation for my work was a fourteen years-long course of Zen training, which brought me face to face with Lao-tzu and his true disciples and heirs, the early Chinese Zen Masters.

With great poetry, the freest translation is sometimes the most faithful. "We must try its effect as an English poem," Dr. Johnson said; "that is the way to judge of the merit of a translation." I have often been fairly literal—or as literal as one *can* be with such a subtle, kaleidoscopic book as the Tao Te Ching. But I have also paraphrased, expanded, contracted, interpreted, worked with the text, played with it, until it became embodied in a language that felt genuine to me. If I haven't always translated Lao-tzu's words, my intention has always been to translate his mind.

Tao Te Ching

The tao that can be told
is not the eternal Tao.
The name that can be named
is not the eternal Name.

The unnamable is the eternally real.
Naming is the origin
of all particular things.

Free from desire, you realize the mystery.
Caught in desire, you see only the manifestations.

Yet mystery and manifestations
arise from the same source.
This source is called darkness.

Darkness within darkness.
The gateway to all understanding.

When people see some things as beautiful,
other things become ugly.
When people see some things as good,
other things become bad.

Being and non-being create each other.
Difficult and easy support each other.
Long and short define each other.
High and low depend on each other.
Before and after follow each other.

Therefore the Master
acts without doing anything
and teaches without saying anything.
Things arise and she lets them come;
things disappear and she lets them go.
She has but doesn't possess,
acts but doesn't expect.
When her work is done, she forgets it.
That is why it lasts forever.

If you overesteem great men,
people become powerless.
If you overvalue possessions,
people begin to steal.

The Master leads
by emptying people's minds
and filling their cores,
by weakening their ambition
and toughening their resolve.
He helps people lose everything
they know, everything they desire,
and creates confusion
in those who think that they know.

Practice not-doing,
and everything will fall into place.

The Tao is like a well:
used but never used up.
It is like the eternal void:
filled with infinite possibilities.

It is hidden but always present.
I don't know who gave birth to it.
It is older than God.

The Tao doesn't take sides;
it gives birth to both good and evil.
The Master doesn't take sides;
she welcomes both saints and sinners.

The Tao is like a bellows:
it is empty yet infinitely capable.
The more you use it, the more it produces;
the more you talk of it, the less you understand.

Hold on to the center.

The Tao is called the Great Mother:
empty yet inexhaustible,
it gives birth to infinite worlds.

It is always present within you.
You can use it any way you want.

The Tao is infinite, eternal.
Why is it eternal?
It was never born;
thus it can never die.
Why is it infinite?
It has no desires for itself;
thus it is present for all beings.

The Master stays behind;
that is why she is ahead.
She is detached from all things;
that is why she is one with them.
Because she has let go of herself,
she is perfectly fulfilled.

The supreme good is like water,
which nourishes all things without trying to.
It is content with the low places that people disdain.
Thus it is like the Tao.

In dwelling, live close to the ground.
In thinking, keep to the simple.
In conflict, be fair and generous.
In governing, don't try to control.
In work, do what you enjoy.
In family life, be completely present.

When you are content to be simply yourself
and don't compare or compete,
everybody will respect you.

Fill your bowl to the brim
and it will spill.
Keep sharpening your knife
and it will blunt.
Chase after money and security
and your heart will never unclench.
Care about people's approval
and you will be their prisoner.

Do your work, then step back.
The only path to serenity.

Can you coax your mind from its wandering
and keep to the original oneness?
Can you let your body become
supple as a newborn child's?
Can you cleanse your inner vision
until you see nothing but the light?
Can you love people and lead them
without imposing your will?
Can you deal with the most vital matters
by letting events take their course?
Can you step back from your own mind
and thus understand all things?

Giving birth and nourishing,
having without possessing,
acting with no expectations,
leading and not trying to control:
this is the supreme virtue.

We join spokes together in a wheel,
but it is the center hole
that makes the wagon move.

We shape clay into a pot,
but it is the emptiness inside
that holds whatever we want.

We hammer wood for a house,
but it is the inner space
that makes it livable.

We work with being,
but non-being is what we use.

Colors blind the eye.
Sounds deafen the ear.
Flavors numb the taste.
Thoughts weaken the mind.
Desires wither the heart.

The Master observes the world
but trusts his inner vision.
He allows things to come and go.
His heart is open as the sky.

Success is as dangerous as failure.
Hope is as hollow as fear.

What does it mean that success is as dangerous as failure?
Whether you go up the ladder or down it,
your position is shaky.
When you stand with your two feet on the ground,
you will always keep your balance.

What does it mean that hope is as hollow as fear?
Hope and fear are both phantoms
that arise from thinking of the self.
When we don't see the self as self,
what do we have to fear?

See the world as your self.
Have faith in the way things are.
Love the world as your self;
then you can care for all things.

Look, and it can't be seen.
Listen, and it can't be heard.
Reach, and it can't be grasped.

Above, it isn't bright.
Below, it isn't dark.
Seamless, unnamable,
it returns to the realm of nothing.
Form that includes all forms,
image without an image,
subtle, beyond all conception.

Approach it and there is no beginning;
follow it and there is no end.
You can't know it, but you can be it,
at ease in your own life.
Just realize where you come from:
this is the essence of wisdom.

The ancient Masters were profound and subtle.
Their wisdom was unfathomable.
There is no way to describe it;
all we can describe is their appearance.

They were careful
as someone crossing an iced-over stream.
Alert as a warrior in enemy territory.
Courteous as a guest.
Fluid as melting ice.
Shapable as a block of wood.
Receptive as a valley.
Clear as a glass of water.

Do you have the patience to wait
till your mud settles and the water is clear?
Can you remain unmoving
till the right action arises by itself?

The Master doesn't seek fulfillment.
Not seeking, not expecting,
she is present, and can welcome all things.

Empty your mind of all thoughts.
Let your heart be at peace.
Watch the turmoil of beings,
but contemplate their return.

Each separate being in the universe
returns to the common source.
Returning to the source is serenity.

If you don't realize the source,
you stumble in confusion and sorrow.
When you realize where you come from,
you naturally become tolerant,
disinterested, amused,
kindhearted as a grandmother,
dignified as a king.
Immersed in the wonder of the Tao,
you can deal with whatever life brings you,
and when death comes, you are ready.

When the Master governs, the people
are hardly aware that he exists.
Next best is a leader who is loved.
Next, one who is feared.
The worst is one who is despised.

If you don't trust the people,
you make them untrustworthy.

The Master doesn't talk, he acts.
When his work is done,
the people say, "Amazing:
we did it, all by ourselves!"

When the great Tao is forgotten,
goodness and piety appear.
When the body's intelligence declines,
cleverness and knowledge step forth.
When there is no peace in the family,
filial piety begins.
When the country falls into chaos,
patriotism is born.

Throw away holiness and wisdom,
and people will be a hundred times happier.
Throw away morality and justice,
and people will do the right thing.
Throw away industry and profit,
and there won't be any thieves.

If these three aren't enough,
just stay at the center of the circle
and let all things take their course.

Stop thinking, and end your problems.
What difference between yes and no?
What difference between success and failure?
Must you value what others value,
avoid what others avoid?
How ridiculous!

Other people are excited,
as though they were at a parade.
I alone don't care,
I alone am expressionless,
like an infant before it can smile.

Other people have what they need;
I alone possess nothing.
I alone drift about,
like someone without a home.
I am like an idiot, my mind is so empty.

Other people are bright;
I alone am dark.
Other people are sharp;
I alone am dull.
Other people have a purpose;
I alone don't know.
I drift like a wave on the ocean,
I blow as aimless as the wind.

I am different from ordinary people.
I drink from the Great Mother's breasts.

The Master keeps her mind
always at one with the Tao;
that is what gives her her radiance.

The Tao is ungraspable.
How can her mind be at one with it?
Because she doesn't cling to ideas.

The Tao is dark and unfathomable.
How can it make her radiant?
Because she lets it.

Since before time and space were,
the Tao is.
It is beyond *is* and *is not*.
How do I know this is true?
I look inside myself and see.

If you want to become whole,
let yourself be partial.
If you want to become straight,
let yourself be crooked.
If you want to become full,
let yourself be empty.
If you want to be reborn,
let yourself die.
If you want to be given everything,
give everything up.

The Master, by residing in the Tao,
sets an example for all beings.
Because he doesn't display himself,
people can see his light.
Because he has nothing to prove,
people can trust his words.
Because he doesn't know who he is,
people recognize themselves in him.
Because he has no goal in mind,
everything he does succeeds.

When the ancient Masters said,
"If you want to be given everything,
give everything up,"
they weren't using empty phrases.
Only in being lived by the Tao
can you be truly yourself.

Express yourself completely,
then keep quiet.
Be like the forces of nature:
when it blows, there is only wind;
when it rains, there is only rain;
when the clouds pass, the sun shines through.

If you open yourself to the Tao,
you are at one with the Tao
and you can embody it completely.
If you open yourself to insight,
you are at one with insight
and you can use it completely.
If you open yourself to loss,
you are at one with loss
and you can accept it completely.

Open yourself to the Tao,
then trust your natural responses;
and everything will fall into place.

He who stands on tiptoe
doesn't stand firm.
He who rushes ahead
doesn't go far.
He who tries to shine
dims his own light.
He who defines himself
can't know who he really is.
He who has power over others
can't empower himself.
He who clings to his work
will create nothing that endures.

If you want to accord with the Tao,
just do your job, then let go.

There was something formless and perfect
before the universe was born.
It is serene. Empty.
Solitary. Unchanging.
Infinite. Eternally present.
It is the mother of the universe.
For lack of a better name,
I call it the Tao.

It flows through all things,
inside and outside, and returns
to the origin of all things.

The Tao is great.
The universe is great.
Earth is great.
Man is great.
These are the four great powers.

Man follows the earth.
Earth follows the universe.
The universe follows the Tao.
The Tao follows only itself.

The heavy is the root of the light.
The unmoved is the source of all movement.

Thus the Master travels all day
without leaving home.
However splendid the views,
she stays serenely in herself.

Why should the lord of the country
flit about like a fool?
If you let yourself be blown to and fro,
you lose touch with your root.
If you let restlessness move you,
you lose touch with who you are.

A good traveler has no fixed plans
and is not intent upon arriving.
A good artist lets his intuition
lead him wherever it wants.
A good scientist has freed himself of concepts
and keeps his mind open to what is.

Thus the Master is available to all people
and doesn't reject anyone.
He is ready to use all situations
and doesn't waste anything.
This is called embodying the light.

What is a good man but a bad man's teacher?
What is a bad man but a good man's job?
If you don't understand this, you will get lost,
however intelligent you are.
It is the great secret.

Know the male,
yet keep to the female:
receive the world in your arms.
If you receive the world,
the Tao will never leave you
and you will be like a little child.

Know the white,
yet keep to the black:
be a pattern for the world.
If you are a pattern for the world,
the Tao will be strong inside you
and there will be nothing you can't do.

Know the personal,
yet keep to the impersonal:
accept the world as it is.
If you accept the world,
the Tao will be luminous inside you
and you will return to your primal self.

The world is formed from the void,
like utensils from a block of wood.
The Master knows the utensils,
yet keeps to the block:
thus she can use all things.

Do you want to improve the world?
I don't think it can be done.

The world is sacred.
It can't be improved.
If you tamper with it, you'll ruin it.
If you treat it like an object, you'll lose it.

There is a time for being ahead,
a time for being behind;
a time for being in motion,
a time for being at rest;
a time for being vigorous,
a time for being exhausted;
a time for being safe,
a time for being in danger.

The Master sees things as they are,
without trying to control them.
She lets them go their own way,
and resides at the center of the circle.

Whoever relies on the Tao in governing men
doesn't try to force issues
or defeat enemies by force of arms.
For every force there is a counterforce.
Violence, even well intentioned,
always rebounds upon oneself.

The Master does his job
and then stops.
He understands that the universe
is forever out of control,
and that trying to dominate events
goes against the current of the Tao.
Because he believes in himself,
he doesn't try to convince others.
Because he is content with himself,
he doesn't need others' approval.
Because he accepts himself,
the whole world accepts him.

Weapons are the tools of violence;
all decent men detest them.

Weapons are the tools of fear;
a decent man will avoid them
except in the direst necessity
and, if compelled, will use them
only with the utmost restraint.
Peace is his highest value.
If the peace has been shattered,
how can he be content?
His enemies are not demons,
but human beings like himself.
He doesn't wish them personal harm.
Nor does he rejoice in victory.
How could he rejoice in victory
and delight in the slaughter of men?

He enters a battle gravely,
with sorrow and with great compassion,
as if he were attending a funeral.

The Tao can't be perceived.
Smaller than an electron,
it contains uncountable galaxies.

If powerful men and women
could remain centered in the Tao,
all things would be in harmony.
The world would become a paradise.
All people would be at peace,
and the law would be written in their hearts.

When you have names and forms,
know that they are provisional.
When you have institutions,
know where their functions should end.
Knowing when to stop,
you can avoid any danger.

All things end in the Tao
as rivers flow into the sea.

Knowing others is intelligence;
knowing yourself is true wisdom.
Mastering others is strength;
mastering yourself is true power.

If you realize that you have enough,
you are truly rich.
If you stay in the center
and embrace death with your whole heart,
you will endure forever.

The great Tao flows everywhere.
All things are born from it,
yet it doesn't create them.
It pours itself into its work,
yet it makes no claim.
It nourishes infinite worlds,
yet it doesn't hold on to them.
Since it is merged with all things
and hidden in their hearts,
it can be called humble.
Since all things vanish into it
and it alone endures,
it can be called great.
It isn't aware of its greatness;
thus it is truly great.

She who is centered in the Tao
can go where she wishes, without danger.
She perceives the universal harmony,
even amid great pain,
because she has found peace in her heart.

Music or the smell of good cooking
may make people stop and enjoy.
But words that point to the Tao
seem monotonous and without flavor.
When you look for it, there is nothing to see.
When you listen for it, there is nothing to hear.
When you use it, it is inexhaustible.

If you want to shrink something,
you must first allow it to expand.
If you want to get rid of something,
you must first allow it to flourish.
If you want to take something,
you must first allow it to be given.
This is called the subtle perception
of the way things are.

The soft overcomes the hard.
The slow overcomes the fast.
Let your workings remain a mystery.
Just show people the results.

The Tao never does anything,
yet through it all things are done.

If powerful men and women
could center themselves in it,
the whole world would be transformed
by itself, in its natural rhythms.
People would be content
with their simple, everyday lives,
in harmony, and free of desire.

When there is no desire,
all things are at peace.

The Master doesn't try to be powerful;
thus he is truly powerful.
The ordinary man keeps reaching for power;
thus he never has enough.

The Master does nothing,
yet he leaves nothing undone.
The ordinary man is always doing things,
yet many more are left to be done.

The kind man does something,
yet something remains undone.
The just man does something,
and leaves many things to be done.
The moral man does something,
and when no one responds
he rolls up his sleeves and uses force.

When the Tao is lost, there is goodness.
When goodness is lost, there is morality.
When morality is lost, there is ritual.
Ritual is the husk of true faith,
the beginning of chaos.

Therefore the Master concerns himself
with the depths and not the surface,
with the fruit and not the flower.
He has no will of his own.
He dwells in reality,
and lets all illusions go.

In harmony with the Tao,
the sky is clear and spacious,
the earth is solid and full,
all creatures flourish together,
content with the way they are,
endlessly repeating themselves,
endlessly renewed.

When man interferes with the Tao,
the sky becomes filthy,
the earth becomes depleted,
the equilibrium crumbles,
creatures become extinct.

The Master views the parts with compassion,
because he understands the whole.
His constant practice is humility.
He doesn't glitter like a jewel
but lets himself be shaped by the Tao,
as rugged and common as a stone.

Return is the movement of the Tao.
Yielding is the way of the Tao.

All things are born of being.
Being is born of non-being.

When a superior man hears of the Tao,
he immediately begins to embody it.
When an average man hears of the Tao,
he half believes it, half doubts it.
When a foolish man hears of the Tao,
he laughs out loud.
If he didn't laugh,
it wouldn't be the Tao.

Thus it is said:
The path into the light seems dark,
the path forward seems to go back,
the direct path seems long,
true power seems weak,
true purity seems tarnished,
true steadfastness seems changeable,
true clarity seems obscure,
the greatest art seems unsophisticated,
the greatest love seems indifferent,
the greatest wisdom seems childish.

The Tao is nowhere to be found.
Yet it nourishes and completes all things.

The Tao gives birth to One.
One gives birth to Two.
Two gives birth to Three.
Three gives birth to all things.

All things have their backs to the female
and stand facing the male.
When male and female combine,
all things achieve harmony.

Ordinary men hate solitude.
But the Master makes use of it,
embracing his aloneness, realizing
he is one with the whole universe.

The gentlest thing in the world
overcomes the hardest thing in the world.
That which has no substance
enters where there is no space.
This shows the value of non-action.

Teaching without words,
performing without actions:
that is the Master's way.

Fame or integrity: which is more important?
Money or happiness: which is more valuable?
Success or failure: which is more destructive?

If you look to others for fulfillment,
you will never truly be fulfilled.
If your happiness depends on money,
you will never be happy with yourself.

Be content with what you have;
rejoice in the way things are.
When you realize there is nothing lacking,
the whole world belongs to you.

True perfection seems imperfect,
yet it is perfectly itself.
True fullness seems empty,
yet it is fully present.

True straightness seems crooked.
True wisdom seems foolish.
True art seems artless.

The Master allows things to happen.
She shapes events as they come.
She steps out of the way
and lets the Tao speak for itself.

When a country is in harmony with the Tao,
the factories make trucks and tractors.
When a country goes counter to the Tao,
warheads are stockpiled outside the cities.

There is no greater illusion than fear,
no greater wrong than preparing to defend yourself,
no greater misfortune than having an enemy.

Whoever can see through all fear
will always be safe.

Without opening your door,
you can open your heart to the world.
Without looking out your window,
you can see the essence of the Tao.

The more you know,
the less you understand.

The Master arrives without leaving,
sees the light without looking,
achieves without doing a thing.

In the pursuit of knowledge,
every day something is added.
In the practice of the Tao,
every day something is dropped.
Less and less do you need to force things,
until finally you arrive at non-action.
When nothing is done,
nothing is left undone.

True mastery can be gained
by letting things go their own way.
It can't be gained by interfering.

The Master has no mind of her own.
She works with the mind of the people.

She is good to people who are good.
She is also good to people who aren't good.
This is true goodness.

She trusts people who are trustworthy.
She also trusts people who aren't trustworthy.
This is true trust.

The Master's mind is like space.
People don't understand her.
They look to her and wait.
She treats them like her own children.

The Master gives himself up
to whatever the moment brings.
He knows that he is going to die,
and he has nothing left to hold on to:
no illusions in his mind,
no resistances in his body.
He doesn't think about his actions;
they flow from the core of his being.
He holds nothing back from life;
therefore he is ready for death,
as a man is ready for sleep
after a good day's work.

Every being in the universe
is an expression of the Tao.
It springs into existence,
unconscious, perfect, free,
takes on a physical body,
lets circumstances complete it.
That is why every being
spontaneously honors the Tao.

The Tao gives birth to all beings,
nourishes them, maintains them,
cares for them, comforts them, protects them,
takes them back to itself,
creating without possessing,
acting without expecting,
guiding without interfering.
That is why love of the Tao
is in the very nature of things.

In the beginning was the Tao.
All things issue from it;
all things return to it.

To find the origin,
trace back the manifestations.
When you recognize the children
and find the mother,
you will be free of sorrow.

If you close your mind in judgments
and traffic with desires,
your heart will be troubled.
If you keep your mind from judging
and aren't led by the senses,
your heart will find peace.

Seeing into darkness is clarity.
Knowing how to yield is strength.
Use your own light
and return to the source of light.
This is called practicing eternity.

The great Way is easy,
yet people prefer the side paths.
Be aware when things are out of balance.
Stay centered within the Tao.

When rich speculators prosper
while farmers lose their land;
when government officials spend money
on weapons instead of cures;
when the upper class is extravagant and irresponsible
while the poor have nowhere to turn—
all this is robbery and chaos.
It is not in keeping with the Tao.

Whoever is planted in the Tao
will not be rooted up.
Whoever embraces the Tao
will not slip away.
Her name will be held in honor
from generation to generation.

Let the Tao be present in your life
and you will become genuine.
Let it be present in your family
and your family will flourish.
Let it be present in your country
and your country will be an example
to all countries in the world.
Let it be present in the universe
and the universe will sing.

How do I know this is true?
By looking inside myself.

He who is in harmony with the Tao
is like a newborn child.
Its bones are soft, its muscles are weak,
but its grip is powerful.
It doesn't know about the union
of male and female,
yet its penis can stand erect,
so intense is its vital power.
It can scream its head off all day,
yet it never becomes hoarse,
so complete is its harmony.

The Master's power is like this.
He lets all things come and go
effortlessly, without desire.
He never expects results;
thus he is never disappointed.
He is never disappointed;
thus his spirit never grows old.

Those who know don't talk.
Those who talk don't know.

Close your mouth,
block off your senses,
blunt your sharpness,
untie your knots,
soften your glare,
settle your dust.
This is the primal identity.

Be like the Tao.
It can't be approached or withdrawn from,
benefited or harmed,
honored or brought into disgrace.
It gives itself up continually.
That is why it endures.

If you want to be a great leader,
you must learn to follow the Tao.
Stop trying to control.
Let go of fixed plans and concepts,
and the world will govern itself.

The more prohibitions you have,
the less virtuous people will be.
The more weapons you have,
the less secure people will be.
The more subsidies you have,
the less self-reliant people will be.

Therefore the Master says:
I let go of the law,
and people become honest.
I let go of economics,
and people become prosperous.
I let go of religion,
and people become serene.
I let go of all desire for the common good,
and the good becomes common as grass.

If a country is governed with tolerance,
the people are comfortable and honest.
If a country is governed with repression,
the people are depressed and crafty.

When the will to power is in charge,
the higher the ideals, the lower the results.
Try to make people happy,
and you lay the groundwork for misery.
Try to make people moral,
and you lay the groundwork for vice.

Thus the Master is content
to serve as an example
and not to impose her will.
She is pointed, but doesn't pierce.
Straightforward, but supple.
Radiant, but easy on the eyes.

For governing a country well
there is nothing better than moderation.

The mark of a moderate man
is freedom from his own ideas.
Tolerant like the sky,
all-pervading like sunlight,
firm like a mountain,
supple like a tree in the wind,
he has no destination in view
and makes use of anything
life happens to bring his way.

Nothing is impossible for him.
Because he has let go,
he can care for the people's welfare
as a mother cares for her child.

Governing a large country
is like frying a small fish.
You spoil it with too much poking.

Center your country in the Tao
and evil will have no power.
Not that it isn't there,
but you'll be able to step out of its way.

Give evil nothing to oppose
and it will disappear by itself.

When a country obtains great power,
it becomes like the sea:
all streams run downward into it.
The more powerful it grows,
the greater the need for humility.
Humility means trusting the Tao,
thus never needing to be defensive.

A great nation is like a great man:
When he makes a mistake, he realizes it.
Having realized it, he admits it.
Having admitted it, he corrects it.
He considers those who point out his faults
as his most benevolent teachers.
He thinks of his enemy
as the shadow that he himself casts.

If a nation is centered in the Tao,
if it nourishes its own people
and doesn't meddle in the affairs of others,
it will be a light to all nations in the world.

The Tao is the center of the universe,
the good man's treasure,
the bad man's refuge.

Honors can be bought with fine words,
respect can be won with good deeds;
but the Tao is beyond all value,
and no one can achieve it.

Thus, when a new leader is chosen,
don't offer to help him
with your wealth or your expertise.
Offer instead
to teach him about the Tao.

Why did the ancient Masters esteem the Tao?
Because, being one with the Tao,
when you seek, you find;
and when you make a mistake, you are forgiven.
That is why everybody loves it.

Act without doing;
work without effort.
Think of the small as large
and the few as many.
Confront the difficult
while it is still easy;
accomplish the great task
by a series of small acts.

The Master never reaches for the great;
thus she achieves greatness.
When she runs into a difficulty,
she stops and gives herself to it.
She doesn't cling to her own comfort;
thus problems are no problem for her.

What is rooted is easy to nourish.
What is recent is easy to correct.
What is brittle is easy to break.
What is small is easy to scatter.

Prevent trouble before it arises.
Put things in order before they exist.
The giant pine tree
grows from a tiny sprout.
The journey of a thousand miles
starts from beneath your feet.

Rushing into action, you fail.
Trying to grasp things, you lose them.
Forcing a project to completion,
you ruin what was almost ripe.

Therefore the Master takes action
by letting things take their course.
He remains as calm
at the end as at the beginning.
He has nothing,
thus has nothing to lose.
What he desires is non-desire;
what he learns is to unlearn.
He simply reminds people
of who they have always been.
He cares about nothing but the Tao.
Thus he can care for all things.

The ancient Masters
didn't try to educate the people,
but kindly taught them to not-know.

When they think that they know the answers,
people are difficult to guide.
When they know that they don't know,
people can find their own way.

If you want to learn how to govern,
avoid being clever or rich.
The simplest pattern is the clearest.
Content with an ordinary life,
you can show all people the way
back to their own true nature.

All streams flow to the sea
because it is lower than they are.
Humility gives it its power.

If you want to govern the people,
you must place yourself below them.
If you want to lead the people,
you must learn how to follow them.

The Master is above the people,
and no one feels oppressed.
She goes ahead of the people,
and no one feels manipulated.
The whole world is grateful to her.
Because she competes with no one,
no one can compete with her.

Some say that my teaching is nonsense.
Others call it lofty but impractical.
But to those who have looked inside themselves,
this nonsense makes perfect sense.
And to those who put it into practice,
this loftiness has roots that go deep.

I have just three things to teach:
simplicity, patience, compassion.
These three are your greatest treasures.
Simple in actions and in thoughts,
you return to the source of being.
Patient with both friends and enemies,
you accord with the way things are.
Compassionate toward yourself,
you reconcile all beings in the world.

The best athlete
wants his opponent at his best.
The best general
enters the mind of his enemy.
The best businessman
serves the communal good.
The best leader
follows the will of the people.

All of them embody
the virtue of non-competition.
Not that they don't love to compete,
but they do it in the spirit of play.
In this they are like children
and in harmony with the Tao.

The generals have a saying:
"Rather than make the first move
it is better to wait and see.
Rather than advance an inch
it is better to retreat a yard."

This is called
going forward without advancing,
pushing back without using weapons.

There is no greater misfortune
than underestimating your enemy.
Underestimating your enemy
means thinking that he is evil.
Thus you destroy your three treasures
and become an enemy yourself.

When two great forces oppose each other,
the victory will go
to the one that knows how to yield.

My teachings are easy to understand
and easy to put into practice.
Yet your intellect will never grasp them,
and if you try to practice them, you'll fail.

My teachings are older than the world.
How can you grasp their meaning?

If you want to know me,
look inside your heart.

Not-knowing is true knowledge.
Presuming to know is a disease.
First realize that you are sick;
then you can move toward health.

The Master is her own physician.
She has healed herself of all knowing.
Thus she is truly whole.

When they lose their sense of awe,
people turn to religion.
When they no longer trust themselves,
they begin to depend upon authority.

Therefore the Master steps back
so that people won't be confused.
He teaches without a teaching,
so that people will have nothing to learn.

The Tao is always at ease.
It overcomes without competing,
answers without speaking a word,
arrives without being summoned,
accomplishes without a plan.

Its net covers the whole universe.
And though its meshes are wide,
it doesn't let a thing slip through.

If you realize that all things change,
there is nothing you will try to hold on to.
If you aren't afraid of dying,
there is nothing you can't achieve.

Trying to control the future
is like trying to take the master carpenter's place.
When you handle the master carpenter's tools,
chances are that you'll cut your hand.

When taxes are too high,
people go hungry.
When the government is too intrusive,
people lose their spirit.

Act for the people's benefit.
Trust them; leave them alone.

Men are born soft and supple;
dead, they are stiff and hard.
Plants are born tender and pliant;
dead, they are brittle and dry.

Thus whoever is stiff and inflexible
is a disciple of death.
Whoever is soft and yielding
is a disciple of life.

The hard and stiff will be broken.
The soft and supple will prevail.

As it acts in the world, the Tao
is like the bending of a bow.
The top is bent downward;
the bottom is bent up.
It adjusts excess and deficiency
so that there is perfect balance.
It takes from what is too much
and gives to what isn't enough.

Those who try to control,
who use force to protect their power,
go against the direction of the Tao.
They take from those who don't have enough
and give to those who have far too much.

The Master can keep giving
because there is no end to her wealth.
She acts without expectation,
succeeds without taking credit,
and doesn't think that she is better
than anyone else.

Nothing in the world
is as soft and yielding as water.
Yet for dissolving the hard and inflexible,
nothing can surpass it.

The soft overcomes the hard;
the gentle overcomes the rigid.
Everyone knows this is true,
but few can put it into practice.

Therefore the Master remains
serene in the midst of sorrow.
Evil cannot enter his heart.
Because he has given up helping,
he is people's greatest help.

True words seem paradoxical.

Failure is an opportunity.
If you blame someone else,
there is no end to the blame.

Therefore the Master
fulfills her own obligations
and corrects her own mistakes.
She does what she needs to do
and demands nothing of others.

If a country is governed wisely,
its inhabitants will be content.
They enjoy the labor of their hands
and don't waste time inventing
labor-saving machines.
Since they dearly love their homes,
they aren't interested in travel.
There may be a few wagons and boats,
but these don't go anywhere.
There may be an arsenal of weapons,
but nobody ever uses them.
People enjoy their food,
take pleasure in being with their families,
spend weekends working in their gardens,
delight in the doings of the neighborhood.
And even though the next country is so close
that people can hear its roosters crowing and its dogs
        barking,
they are content to die of old age
without ever having gone to see it.

True words aren't eloquent;
eloquent words aren't true.
Wise men don't need to prove their point;
men who need to prove their point aren't wise.

The Master has no possessions.
The more he does for others,
the happier he is.
The more he gives to others,
the wealthier he is.

The Tao nourishes by not forcing.
By not dominating, the Master leads.

Notes

CHAPTER 1

Describing the indescribable, teaching the unteachable, pointing the way to the Way—what does Lao-tzu think he is doing here? It can't be done. No way.

Hence Po Chü-i, poet and stand-up comedian, wrote,

> "He who talks doesn't know,
> he who knows doesn't talk":
> that is what Lao-tzu told us,
> in a book of five thousand words.
> If he was the one who knew,
> how could he have been such a blabbermouth?

That's the problem with spiritual teachers. They *have* to be blabbermouths. But their words are (in the traditional Buddhist metaphor) fingers pointing at the moon; if you watch the finger, you can't see the moon. How meticulous the great Masters had to be!

> A monk asked Ma-tzu, "Why do you teach, 'Mind is Buddha'?"
>
> Ma-tzu said, "To stop a baby from crying."
>
> The monk said, "When the crying has stopped, what then?"
>
> Ma-tzu said, "Then I teach, 'Not mind, not Buddha.' "
>
> The monk said, "How about someone who isn't attached to either?"
>
> Ma-tzu said, "I would tell him, 'Not beings.' "
>
> The monk said, "And what if you met a man unattached to all things: what would you tell *him?*"

Ma-tzu said, "I would just let him experience the great Tao."

In fact, the truth is right before our eyes; right under our noses; so simple that every child understands it; and yet, as Bankei said, the farther you enter into it, the deeper it is. Where is the way to the Way? What a question!

Still, for complicated minds, drastic measures are needed. Lao-tzu's book was written as a response, out of grandmotherly kindness. According to the oldest biography,

> Lao-tzu lived for a long time in the country of Chou, but seeing its decline he departed. When he reached the frontier, the guard said, "Since you are going away, Sir, could you write a book to teach me the art of living?" Thereupon Lao-tzu wrote his book about the Tao, and departed.

This is legend, but it is an accurate description of the way in which true teaching happens. He who knows doesn't talk, but words are no hindrance for him. He uses them as he would use gardening tools. When someone asks, he answers.

The tao that can be told / is not the eternal Tao: The text reads, "The tao that can be tao-ed [one meaning of *tao* being 'to express'] / is not the eternal Tao." Other possible renderings: "The way that can be weighed / is not the eternal Way," "The force that can be forced / is not the eternal Force."

you realize the mystery: Infinitely marvelous, yet as ordinary as sunlight. Impossible to know, yet as easy as touching your nose when you wash your face.

This source is called darkness: Because none of our senses can perceive it. It is also called "light," because the less we obstruct it, the more radiant we are.

The gateway to all understanding: In order to understand, we have to remain in the darkness of not-knowing.

CHAPTER 2

acts without doing anything: Her actions are appropriate responses. Thus they are effortless. She embodies compassion, yet she doesn't try to be compassionate. She doesn't struggle to make money, yet she enjoys spending it when it comes to her. She goes her own way, yet she accepts help gratefully and has no pride in walking alone. She is not elated by praise, not discouraged by neglect. She doesn't give even a moment's thought to right or wrong. She never has to make a decision; decisions arise by themselves. She is like an actress who loves her role. The Tao is writing the script.

teaches without saying anything: The way she buys oranges or ties her shoelaces is a teaching. Her face is more eloquent than any scripture could be.

That is why it lasts forever: Not in time and space, but in quality.

CHAPTER 3

emptying people's minds: He empties them of concepts, judgments, and desires. Thus they can return to a state of childlike simplicity.

filling their cores: He fills them with a sense of their original identity. Thus they can return to a state of joy.

weakening their ambition: When they have no false self to nourish or defend, they find that greed, hatred, and arrogance vanish by themselves.

toughening their resolve: Their innermost intention. They develop enough self-reliance to give up the idea of self.

CHAPTER 4

Following Ch'en Ku-ying, I have deleted the second stanza of the Chinese text, which seems to be an interpolation from chapter 56.

It is older than God: There is no God when there is nothing *but* God.

CHAPTER 5

The Tao doesn't take sides; / it gives birth to both good and evil: Literally, "Heaven and earth are impartial; they treat all things like straw dogs," as the Master "treats all people like straw dogs." Straw dogs were ritual objects, venerated before the ceremony but afterward abandoned and trampled underfoot. The point here is not that the Tao is cruel to things, nor that the Master is ruthless with people, but that they are impartial. The Master sees all beings arising from the same source, working out their karma (usually with great suffering), and returning to the source. And since people are in constant flux, she understands that at any moment they are capable of the most astonishing spiritual transformations. Why should she pin them motionless with a judgment of "good" or "bad"?

CHAPTER 6

First stanza: Literally, "The spirit of the valley never dies. It is called the mysterious female. The gate of the mysterious female is the root of heaven and earth." Chu Hsi said,

"The female is one who receives something and, with it, creates. This creative principle is the most marvelous thing in the universe."

CHAPTER 7

The Tao is infinite, eternal: Here is everywhere. Anytime is now.

The Master stays behind; that is why she is ahead: She is like a turtle: wherever she is, is home. Actually, she is neither behind nor ahead, but exactly even with all things.

She is detached: Bunan said, "It is easy to keep things at a distance; it is hard to be naturally beyond them." Detachment results in clarity; clarity expresses itself in love. Her heart is like a mirror, which reflects all faces, without judgment, exactly as they are.

CHAPTER 8

The supreme good is like water: I asked my friend and teacher Emilie Conrad-Da'oud, founder of Continuum, to comment on this verse. She said,

> Water is the source of all life, life's matrix and fecundity; it overflows into everything, it moves everywhere. We are fundamentally water: muscled water. And the idea that we ever leave the amniotic fluid is a misconception. The amniotic fluid is the state of total nourishment and unconditional love. It is always present for us and contains everything we could possibly want. In fact, we *are* that fluid of love.

CHAPTER 9

Do your work, then step back: When you do your work wholeheartedly, you are glad to let it go, just as a parent lets a child go, into its own life.

CHAPTER 10

Can you let your body become: Literally, "Can you concentrate
your *ch'i* [vital energy] until it becomes . . ."

supple as a newborn child's: Emilie Conrad-Da'oud's
comment·

> There is no self-consciousness in the newborn child.
> Later on, the mind wanders into self-images, starts to
> think *Should I do this? Is this movement right?* and loses the
> immediacy of the moment. As self-consciousness de-
> velops, the muscles become less supple, less like the
> world. But the young child is pure fluidity. It isn't
> aware of any separation, so all its movements are spon-
> taneous and alive and whole and perfect.
>
> If an adult body becomes truly supple, though,
> there's a quality to its movement that the child's doesn't
> have, a texture of experience, a fourth dimension of
> time. When we watch a seventy-year-old hand move,
> we feel, "Yes, that hand has lived." All the bodies it has
> touched, all the weights it has lifted, all the heads it has
> cradled are present in its movement. It is resonant with
> experience; the fingers curve with a sense of having
> been there. Whereas in a child's hand there's a sense of
> just arriving. The child's movement is pristine and in-
> nocent and delightful, but a truly supple adult move-
> ment is awesome, because all life is included in it.

until you see nothing but the light: That is, until your heart
is at peace. The great modern Indian sage Ramana Maharshi said,

> There is no greater mystery than this, that we keep
> seeking reality though in fact we *are* reality. We think
> that there is something hiding our reality and that this
> must be destroyed before reality is gained. How ridic-

ulous! A day will dawn when you will laugh at all your past efforts. That which will be on the day you laugh is also here and now.

Can you love people and lead them / without imposing your will: Emilie Conrad-Da'oud's comment:

The more supple your body is, the less dictatorial you'll be. The military stance is the most invasive stance that you can possibly take. Its opposite—the boneless, wishy-washy posture of someone who doesn't stand for anything—is just as unhealthy. Suppleness is really fluidity. It transcends strength and weakness. When your body is supple, it feels like there's no barrier in you, you can flow in any direction, your movement is a complete expression of yourself.

by letting events take their course: Literally, "by becoming the female." The Ho-shang Kung commentary says, "In arranging one's life properly, one should be as calm and flexible as a woman."

CHAPTER 11

non-being is what we use: The true teacher realizes that there is nothing to teach; that's why he can teach anyone who wants to learn. The true lover realizes that there is no one to love; that's why he is available to anyone who needs him. The Master realizes that there is nowhere to stand; that's why he can stand anywhere.

CHAPTER 12

Colors blind the eye, etc.: We need space in order to see, silence in order to hear, sleep in order to carry on with our wakefulness. If the senses are too cluttered with objects, they lose their acuteness and will eventually decay.

Desires wither the heart: Once it has let go of desires, the heart naturally overflows with love, like David's cup in Psalm 23.

his inner vision: There is no inside or outside for him. He reflects whatever appears, without judgment, whether it is a flower or a heap of garbage, a criminal or a saint. Whatever happens is all right. He treats his own anger or grief just as he would treat an angry or grieving child: with compassion.

open as the sky: The sky holds sun, moon, stars, clouds, rain, snow, or pure azure. Because it doesn't care which of these appear, it has room for them all.

CHAPTER 13

keep your balance: The trick is to go up or down the ladder *with* your feet on the ground. Bravo! Bravissimo!!

See the world as your self: The outer mirrors the inner.

CHAPTER 14

Look, and it can't be seen: Another way of saying this: "Look, and it's right before your eyes."

CHAPTER 15

till your mud settles: "Mud" stands for concepts, judgments, desires, expectations—everything that obscures and narrows reality. The Master's life is pure and placid: predictable like the seasons, obvious like the moon. When our mind/heart becomes transparent, the light of the Tao shines through.

the water is clear: I asked my old teacher, Zen Master Seung Sahn, to comment on this verse. He said,

Our mind is like a glass of clear water. If we put salt into the water, it becomes salt water; sugar, it becomes sugar water; shit, it becomes shit water. But originally the water is clear. No thinking, no mind. No mind, no problem.

CHAPTER 16

Empty your mind: This doesn't mean "suppress your thoughts," but "step back from them." Insight into the Tao has nothing to do with the intellect and its abstractions. When we step out of self-consciousness, we step into the Tao. Lin Ching-hsi said,

> The mind is originally empty, and only when it remains empty, without grasping or rejecting, can it respond to natural things, without prejudice. It should be like a river gorge with a swan flying overhead; the river has no desire to retain the swan, yet the swan's passage is traced by its shadow, without any omission. Another example: A mirror will reflect all things perfectly, whether they are beautiful or ugly; it never refuses to show a thing, nor does it retain the thing after it is gone. The mind should be as open as this.

Does this sound anti-intellectual? But listen to Einstein:

> The scientist's religious feeling takes the form of a rapturous amazement at the harmony of natural law, which reveals an intelligence of such superiority that, in comparison with it, all the systematic thinking of human beings is an utterly insignificant reflection. This feeling is the guiding principle of his life and work.

93

CHAPTER 17

One of several chapters that are as relevant to child-rearing as to government.

The Master doesn't talk, he acts: His words are in perfect harmony with his actions. He is always genuine.

CHAPTER 18

the great Tao: Jayata said to Vasubandu, "If you have nothing to ask for in your mind, that state of mind is called the Tao."

goodness and piety appear: When the Tao is forgotten, people act according to rules, not from the heart. This goodness is as insecure as Job's and can be as self-satisfied as Little Jack Horner's. Whereas a good father has no intention of being good; he just acts naturally.

CHAPTER 19

throw away holiness and wisdom: When some folks are called saints, other folks think of themselves as sinners. When one fellow is called wise, others imagine that there is something they need to know. The Master doesn't have these categories; for her, no one is wise or holy; thus, in her presence everyone feels at home.

CHAPTER 20

yes and no:

Chao-chou asked Nan-ch'üan, "What is the Tao?"
Nan-ch'üan said, "Everyday mind is the Tao."
Chao-chou said, "How can I approach it?"
Nan-ch'üan said, "The more you try to approach it, the farther away you'll be."
"But if I don't get close, how can I understand it?"

The Master said, "It's not a question of understanding or not understanding. Understanding is delusion; not understanding is indifference. But when you reach the unattainable Tao, it is like pure space, limitless and serene. Where is there room in it for yes or no?"

I alone don't care: If good happens, good; if bad happens, good.

I am like an idiot: First you erase the blackboard; then you can write something new.

I am different from ordinary people: I am more ordinary. When I am hungry, I eat; when I am tired, I sleep; that's all. Pai-chang said,

> After enlightenment one is still the same as one was before. One is simply free from unreality and delusion. The ordinary person's mind is the same as the sage's, because Original Mind is perfect and complete in itself. After you have had this recognition, please don't lose it.

CHAPTER 21

before time and space: Philo said, "Today means boundless and inexhaustible eternity. Months and years and all periods of time are concepts of men, who gauge everything by number; but the true name of eternity is Today."

CHAPTER 22

If you want to become whole, etc.: Unless you accept yourself, you can't let go of yourself.

Because he doesn't know who he is: From the standpoint of personality, he knows very well who he is; that is what allows him to use his personality for people's benefit, rather than be used by it. But from the standpoint of his true self, there is nowhere to stand and no self to know. He doesn't know; he just is.

Only in being lived by the Tao: This is what Paul of Tarsus meant by, "Not I, but Christ in me." Or, in a more light-hearted vein, the little boy who when his mother got annoyed and said "Stop sneezing!" answered, "I'm *not* sneezing! *It's* sneezing *me!*"

CHAPTER 23
trust your natural responses: Trust the intelligence of the body.

CHAPTER 24
power over others: The other *is* the self. When we understand this, we are able to use power wisely.

CHAPTER 25
mother of the universe: As chapter 51 says, "The Tao gives birth to all beings, / nourishes them, maintains them, / cares for them, comforts them, protects them, / takes them back to itself."

These are the four great powers: Ho-hum.

CHAPTER 26
without leaving home: She never loses touch with who she really is. In the midst of joy or anger or sorrow, she remains imperturbable.

CHAPTER 27
This is one of the most important chapters in the Tao Te Ching.

First stanza: I have been very free here, because the central point—openness to reality, openheartedness—needs to be made as clearly as possible. The original text reads:

A good walker leaves no traces or tracks. A good speaker makes no slips or errors. A good calculator needs no counting-sticks or tallies. A good locksmith uses no bolts or keys, yet no one can open. A good binder uses no ropes or cords, yet no one can loosen.

available to all people: Because he is not attached to his own ideas.

you will get lost: In moral judgments. The Tree of the Knowledge of Good and Evil is the Tree of Death.

CHAPTER 28
Know the male, / yet keep to the female: Keeping to the receptive allows the creative to arise. Actually, the creative and the receptive are complementary sides of the same process.

CHAPTER 29
Do you want to improve the world: Ramana Maharshi said,

Wanting to reform the world without discovering one's true self is like trying to cover the world with leather to avoid the pain of walking on stones and thorns. It is much simpler to wear shoes.

It can't be improved: This is the Sabbath mind, as in the first chapter of Genesis: when God, from a state of perfect repose, looks at the world and says, "Behold, it is very good." Actually, this "it can't be improved" is the greatest possible improvement. Compare chapter 35: "She perceives the universal harmony, / even amid great pain, / because she has found peace in her heart."

doesn't try to force issues: He lets the issues resolve themselves.

    out of control: Out of the control of his own, tiny, personal, conscious self.

CHAPTER 31

Peace is his highest value: Peace means wholeness.

CHAPTER 32

Smaller than an electron: Neither small nor large. Neither here nor there. Neither past nor future nor present. Also (as long as we're discussing this) all of the above.

CHAPTER 33

true wisdom: When I know myself, I know others. When I master myself, I don't need to master others.

CHAPTER 34

it doesn't create them: It is more like a mother than like an artisan, giving birth rather than making. It acts without any conscious plan or purpose. God doesn't say, "Let there be light." The light simply is, and is God.

CHAPTER 35

peace in her heart: She is centered in the peace; thus she can give herself fully to the pain.

    without flavor: Zen Master Seung Sahn's comment:

> The Great Way has no gate.
> Clear water has no taste.
> The tongue has no bone.
> In complete stillness, a stone girl is dancing.

CHAPTER 36

If you want to shrink something: For example, defects in your character. When suppressed or ignored, they continue; but when allowed to be present in your awareness, they eventually wither away. Or, as Blake said from a slightly different perspective, "The road of excess leads to the palace of wisdom."

CHAPTER 37

If powerful men and women / could center themselves in it: They can!

CHAPTER 38

The Master does nothing: He has no goal in mind, doesn't think that *he* is doing anything. He's just along for the ride.

yet he leaves nothing undone: No expectations. No regrets. No residue.

When the Tao is lost: You can never lose the Tao. But you can find it.

Therefore the Master concerns himself / with the depths and not the surface: In the depths, there is no distinction between depths and surface. Fruit in autumn, flowers in spring. He enjoys the flowers, as he enjoys the fruit.

CHAPTER 39

lets himself be shaped by the Tao: As a piece of marble lets itself be shaped by the sculptor, so that the statue inside can be revealed. Hammer and chisel are necessary agents. Ouch.

CHAPTER 40

Being is born of non-being: "Non-being" means beyond the categories of being and non-being.

the greatest love seems indifferent: Because it has no preferences. A good father loves all his children equally, whether
they turn out to be thieves or carpenters or messiahs. As Jesus of Nazareth said, "Love your enemies [i.e., treat them
with generosity and compassion], so that you may be children of your father in heaven: for he makes his sun rise on
the evil and on the good, and sends his rain on the just and
on the unjust."

CHAPTER 42

The Tao gives birth to One: When it's called One, it is no
longer the Tao. (When it's called the Tao, it is no longer the
Tao.)

    One gives birth to Two: Oy!

    Two gives birth to Three: Where will it end?

    Three gives birth to all things: I knew it! Now once more
from the top, with feeling.

    All things have their backs to the female, etc.: Literally, "The
ten thousand things carry [at their backs] the *yin* and embrace [in front] the *yang*; through the blending of the energy [*ch'i*] of these two, they achieve harmony."

    Last stanza: I have improvised here. The text reads:

> People hate to be orphans, widowers, starvelings. Yet
> kings and princes take these names as their titles.
> Therefore sometimes you gain by losing; sometimes
> you lose by gaining. What others have taught, I teach
> also: 'The violent will not die a natural death.' I will
> make this the father of my teaching.

gentlest . . . / hardest . . . : Examples: water and rock, love
and hostility.

CHAPTER 44

Fame or integrity, etc.: But why be caught in these dichotomies? Once he has surrendered to the Tao, the Master accepts whatever comes to him. If fame comes, he uses it with integrity. If money comes, he uses it as pure energy. Success and failure are equally irrelevant to him, because his heart rests in the Tao.

CHAPTER 45

True perfection: A cracked coffee cup. The sound of traffic outside your window.

True fullness: Attention, for example.

CHAPTER 46

Whoever can see through all fear: This is the only *real* defense. President Roosevelt said, "We have nothing to fear but fear itself." I would say, "Not even that."

CHAPTER 47

The more you know: The more you know without knowing yourself.

CHAPTER 48

every day something is dropped: Gratefully.

True mastery can be gained: Actually, it can't be gained. True mastery *is* letting things take their course.

CHAPTER 49

The Master has no mind of her own: She has a strong will and a strong character, but she is permeable. And her mind is so subtle that, in comparison with the rigid thought- and desire-structures of other people, it seems to be pure space.

She also trusts people who aren't trustworthy: Like a parent whose child has broken a rule. Of course, if a parent is genuine, the child will be genuine too.

CHAPTER 50

There are a number of passages in the Tao Te Ching where a much narrower consciousness is at work than in the rest of the book. These passages may be interpolations (several show a concern with immortality, as the later, magical Taoism did). Or perhaps the old fellow had indigestion on the days he wrote them. But since my job was to recreate the essential mind of Lao-tzu, I could not in good conscience include them in this version. What I have done instead is to make improvisations on the passage's theme, always taking care to remain within the consciousness and language of the main body of the text. For those who are curious, I have included literal translations in these notes.

The text here reads:

Coming in is life; going out is death. Three in ten are companions of life; three in ten are companions of death. And three in ten are moving from life to the place of death. Why is this? Because they live life too intensely. I have heard that he who knows how to preserve his life meets neither rhinoceros nor tiger when he travels by land, and is untouched by the sword when he enters a battle. The rhinoceros finds no place in him to drive its horn; the tiger finds no place in him to sink its claws; the soldier finds no place in him to thrust his sword. Why is this? Because in him there is no place of death.

he has nothing left: Zen Master Seung Sahn's comment:

Coming in emptyhanded,
going out emptyhanded.
What is your original face?
The moon is shining everywhere.

CHAPTER 51

spontaneously honors the Tao: Honoring the Tao means respecting the way things are. There is a wonderful Japanese story (adapted here from Zenkei Shibayama Roshi's *A Flower Does Not Talk*) which portrays this attitude:

A hundred and fifty years ago there lived a woman named Sono, whose devotion and purity of heart were respected far and wide. One day a fellow Buddhist, having made a long trip to see her, asked, "What can I do to put my heart at rest?" She said, "Every morning and every evening, and whenever anything happens to you, keep on saying, 'Thanks for everything. I have no complaint whatsoever.' " The man did as he was instructed, for a whole year, but his heart was still not at peace. He returned to Sono, crestfallen. "I've said your prayer over and over, and yet nothing in my life has changed; I'm still the same selfish person as before. What should I do now?" Sono immediately said, " 'Thanks for everything. I have no complaint whatsoever.' " On hearing these words, the man was able to open his spiritual eye, and returned home with a great joy.

CHAPTER 52

trace back the manifestations: Where do you come from?

CHAPTER 53

The great Way is easy: Zen Master Seng-ts'an said,

The great Way is not difficult
if you don't cling to good and bad.
Just let go of your preferences:
and everything will be perfectly clear.

CHAPTER 54

genuine: The mark of a genuine person is straightforward-
ness. He has nothing to hide, nothing to defend.

CHAPTER 55

like a newborn child: Chuang-tzu said,

> The infant cries all day long without straining its
> throat. It clenches its fist all day long without cramping
> its hand. It stares all day long without weakening its
> eyes. Free from all worries, unaware of itself, it acts
> without thinking, doesn't know why things happen,
> doesn't need to know.

The Master's power is like this, etc.: I have improvised here.
The text reads:

> To know harmony is to know the eternal; to know the
> eternal is to have insight. To improve upon life is omi-
> nous; to control the *ch'i* by the mind is aggressiveness.
> When they are too aggressive, things decay. This is
> non-Tao. Non-Tao soon ends.

CHAPTER 56

Those who know don't talk: They don't talk for the sake of
talking, or to prove something, or to display themselves.
They talk only if it's appropriate (and if they feel like
talking).

Those who talk don't know: This is ignorance, not the
openness of not-knowing.

CHAPTER 57

the world will govern itself: Just as Nature regulates itself, without any need of our bright ideas.

CHAPTER 58

Second stanza: I have improvised here. The text reads:

> Prosperity rests on disaster; disaster is hidden in prosperity. Who knows the line that separates them? The normal becomes the perverted, the good becomes the monstrous. People have long been confused about this.

CHAPTER 59

I have improvised here. The text reads:

> In governing people and serving heaven, nothing is better than moderation. Only he who is moderate can prepare in advance. He who prepares in advance accumulates a reserve of *te* [virtue or power; the Tao as it informs things and acts in the world]. He who accumulates a reserve of *te* overcomes all obstacles. He who overcomes all obstacles has no limits. He who has no limits can possess a country. He who possesses the mother of a country can keep it for a long time. This is called having deep roots and a strong stem, long life and enduring vision.

CHAPTER 60

step out of its way: It will be like a sword cutting the air. No harm.

CHAPTER 61

I have improvised here. The text reads:

A large country is like the lower part of a river. It is the meeting-point of the universe, the female of the universe. The female, by tranquility, conquers the male. By tranquility she takes the lower position. Therefore a large country by placing itself in a lower position can conquer a small country. A small country by being in a lower position can conquer a large country. Therefore the one conquers by placing itself lower, the other conquers by being naturally lower. A large country wants nothing more than to gather people and nourish them. A small country wants nothing more than to enter and serve the people. Since both get what they want, the large country should take the lower position.

CHAPTER 62

The Tao is the center of the universe: The center is everywhere.

the good man's treasure: It is like the magic purse: he can spend it freely, and there is always more.

the bad man's refuge: It doesn't judge him. Thus he can step outside his idea of himself. There is always another chance.

no one can achieve it: Because there is no "it."

Offer instead / to teach him about the Tao: Better yet, *don't* offer. The Master simply responds to circumstances in the appropriate way. If the President or the Pope or a border guard has a question, he will be glad to answer it. Otherwise, he minds his business and leaves everything to the Tao.

CHAPTER 63

When she runs into a difficulty: A difficulty is like a letter with her address on it.

CHAPTER 64

He cares about nothing but the Tao: Which is not to say that he doesn't love his wife, children, friends, country, planet. But he sees them in the proper perspective: of eternity. And since he and his wife love the Tao even more than they love each other, their marriage is radiant with love. This is the meaning of the Biblical verse "You shall love the Unnamable your God with all your heart, with all your soul, and with all your strength."

CHAPTER 65

kindly taught them to not-know: The ancient Masters taught them the supreme value of Don't-know Mind, which is forever fresh, open, and fertile with possibilities. (Another name for it is Beginner's Mind.)

CHAPTER 66

The Master is above the people: Not that she feels superior, but that, looking from a higher vantage point, she can see more.

The whole world is grateful to her: Even those who think they are ungrateful.

no one can compete with her: She sees everyone as her equal.

CHAPTER 67

Second stanza: I have improvised here. The text reads:

> I have three treasures which I preserve and treasure. The first is compassion, the second is frugality, the third is daring not to be first in the world. Whoever has compassion can be brave. Whoever has frugality can be generous. Whoever dares not to be first in the world can become the leader of the world. But to be brave without compassion, generous without frugality, prominent

without humility: this is fatal. Whoever shows compassion in battle will conquer. Whoever shows compassion in defense will stand firm. Heaven helps and protects those with compassion.

CHAPTER 68

I have improvised here. The text reads:

A skillful officer isn't warlike. A skillful fighter isn't violent. A skillful conqueror isn't competitive. A skillful employer places himself below others. This is called the *te* of not competing. This is called the power to use men's abilities. This is called complying with heaven. Since ancient times it has been the best way.

CHAPTER 69

Underestimating your enemy: Even thinking of him as an enemy is dangerous. If you need a word, use "opponent." May the best man (as they say) win.

CHAPTER 70

easy to put into practice: Grasses and trees have no trouble with it; animals are perfect disciples.

look inside your heart: And keep looking. Keep listening, too, until the sights and the sounds disappear by themselves.

CHAPTER 71

First realize that you are sick: Novalis said, "We are close to waking up when we dream that we are dreaming."

CHAPTER 72

Therefore the Master steps back: He doesn't act as guru or messiah, because he doesn't want to keep people dependent on him, and thus spiritually immature. When people start to treat him like a holy man, he nips their adoration in the bud and points them to their inner messiah.

people will have nothing to learn: They just need to *un*learn.

CHAPTER 73
The Tao is always at ease: At ease with herself, the Master puts everyone else at ease.

CHAPTER 74
Trying to control the future: Thinking that you know what is good or bad, what is advantageous or harmful. The *Huai Nan Tzu* tells a story about this:

> A poor farmer's horse ran off into the country of the barbarians. All his neighbors offered their condolences, but his father said, "How do you know that this isn't good fortune?" After a few months the horse returned with a barbarian horse of excellent stock. All his neighbors offered their congratulations, but his father said, "How do you know that this isn't a disaster?" The two horses bred, and the family became rich in fine horses. The farmer's son spent much of his time riding them; one day he fell off and broke his hipbone. All his neighbors offered the farmer their condolences, but his father said, "How do you know that this isn't good fortune?" Another year passed, and the barbarians invaded the frontier. All the able-bodied young men were conscripted, and nine-tenths of them died in the war. Thus good fortune can be disaster and vice versa. Who can tell how events will be transformed?

CHAPTER 75
leave them alone: Offer them the gift of not being dependent on you.

CHAPTER 76

disciple of life: The less rigid, the readier for life *or* death.

CHAPTER 77

and doesn't think that she is better: She is simply more transparent.

CHAPTER 78

he is people's greatest help: The greatest help is wholeheartedly trusting people to resolve their own problems. A true philanthropist, like a good parent, brings people to the point where they can help themselves.

True words seem paradoxical: Only when the mind is cluttered with untruth.

CHAPTER 79

If you blame someone else: Confucius said,

> In the archer there is a resemblance to the mature person. When he misses the mark, he turns and seeks the reason for his failure in himself.

CHAPTER 80

without ever having gone to see it: Not that they are lacking in appropriate curiosity. But they have their priorities straight.

CHAPTER 81

The Master has no possessions: These no-possessions may include a house, a car, a computer, a roomful of books, and an electric toothbrush.

The more he does for others, / the happier he is: Because he is doing it for himself.

The more he gives to others, / the wealthier he is: The less he holds on to, the more he can give himself to others. When he can give himself completely, his wealth is infinite.

Acknowledgments

Lao Tzu: Text, Notes, and Comments by Ch'en Ku-ying (Chinese Materials Center, 1981) furnished help on textual matters and commentaries. Of the many translations that I consulted, Liou Kia-Hway's *Tao Tö King* (Gallimard, 1967) was particularly useful. Occasionally I have borrowed a phrase from the translation of Gia-fu Feng and Jane English (Vintage, 1972).

John Tarrant, Jane Hirshfield, Jacob Needleman, and Robert Aitken Roshi read the manuscript and made helpful suggestions.

For his considerable share in the making of this book, I would like to express my deep gratitude to that prince among agents, my friend Michael Katz.

About the Translator

Stephen Mitchell was born in Brooklyn, New York, in 1943, and studied at Amherst, the University of Paris, and Yale. His books include *Dropping Ashes on the Buddha*, *The Selected Poetry of Rainer Maria Rilke*, *The Book of Job*, *The Enlightened Heart*, *Parables and Portraits*, *The Enlightened Mind*, and *The Gospel According to Jesus*. He lives with his wife, Vicki Chang, an acupuncturist and healer, in northern California.